A TASTE OF HEBREW

A Do-It-Yourself Hebrew Primer for Adults

Prequel to *Aleph Isn't Tough*

AARON L. STARR

There are so many people deserving of thanks for bringing this book to fruition that the list would be a book in and of itself. Suffice it to say, thank you to all who have shared their passion for learning and teaching with me over the years. More specifically, thank you to Rabbi Marc Gruber for his insight, wisdom, and constant encouragement toward developing this curriculum. Thank you to Rabbi Hara Person for her support, faith, and creativity in making this book a reality, and to everyone else at the URJ Press, including Ron Ghatan, Victor Ney, Zack Kolstein, and Lauren Dubin.

And finally, thank you to Rebecca—my favorite teacher, my best friend, and my beloved.

Welcome to *A Taste of Hebrew*! While you may use this book in many different ways, I suggest the following route:

1. Start by looking at the **letter in the middle of the page**. What is its name? What does it look like to you? What might help you to connect the sound of the letter with the appearance of the letter?

2. Go next to the upper left-hand corner for **Commentators' Corner**. Here you will find interesting tidbits about how that Hebrew letter is used in the Jewish tradition. Perhaps this information will help you to remember the name, sound, and appearance of the letter.

3. In the upper right-hand corner is the **Vital Vowels** section. Like any language, vowels help to connect consonants. In Hebrew, most vowels are located underneath the letter.

4. **T'filah Tidbits** is in the bottom right-hand corner. This information can help you to better identify the letter you are learn-ing, and it can deepen your comfort level in the prayer service by explaining various prayers that Jews say.

5. In the bottom left-hand corner you will find some **practice exercises** to help cement your learning of the Hebrew letter and vowel on the page. Sometimes these words are just made up for the sake of learning; sometimes they are real words to help build your Hebrew vocabulary. On the reverse side of each page are **pronunciation tools** to serve as an answer key to the exercises, as well as more opportunities for you to practice reading.

6. Smile and enjoy! Learning a language can be difficult at any age or stage. Yet, by choosing this sacred path, I am sure you will deepen your connection to Judaism; to your fellow Jews of yesterday, today, and tomorrow; and to God. I wish you *hatzlachah rabbah*: much success on your Hebrew journey!

Rabbi Aaron Starr

Commentators' Corner

The Rabbis ask why the first two words of the Torah begin with the second letter of the Hebrew alphabet, ב, instead of the first letter, *aleph*, א. The Rabbis answer their own question by suggesting that God wanted the Torah to begin with a letter of blessing. Since the Hebrew word for "blessing" is *b'rachah* (beginning with a ב), God decided to begin the Torah with *B'reishit bara*, or "In the beginning, God created..." (*B'reishit Rabbah* 1:10), both words that begin with the letter ב. What does the Creation story teach about how we should treat the environment?

Exercises

Remember Hebrew is read from right to left.

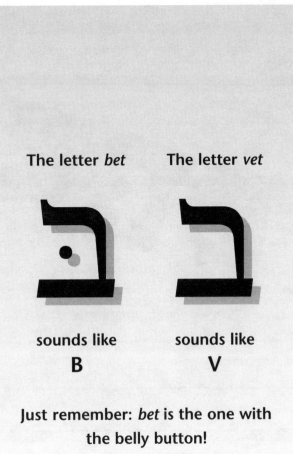

The letter *bet*

The letter *vet*

sounds like
B

sounds like
V

Just remember: *bet* is the one with the belly button!

בְּ   בְּ   בְּ   ⬅

בְּ   בְּ   בְּ   ⬅

(See back for answers.)

Vital Vowels

Note: Hebrew vowels are usually placed beneath the consonant.

Kamatz: ָ

The *kamatz* makes an "ah" sound, like in the English words "FAther" or "BOther," or in the Hebrew word *baruch*. In transliteration, it is denoted by the letter *a*.

T'filah Tidbits

ב is the first letter of the Hebrew root that means "bless." For example, *b'rachah* means "a blessing," and this word is related to the first word of most of our prayers, *baruch*, which means "blessed" or "praised." This Hebrew root lends itself to the name of the first prayer of the main body of the prayer service, the *Bar'chu*. The prayer leader calls us to worship by saying, *Bar'chu et Adonai ham'vorach*, or "Praise the Eternal to whom praise is due!" The congregation responds, *Baruch Adonai ham'vorach l'olam va-ed*, "Praised be the Eternal to whom praise is due, now and forever!" The prayer immediately following the *Bar'chu* is a prayer thanking God for the beauty of creation. It also begins with the ב, for *baruch*. If you wanted to start saying one *b'rachah* (blessing) a day, what would it be?

Transliteration and Answer Key	תַּרְגוּם Translation	תַּרְגִּילִים בְּעִבְרִית Hebrew Exercises
ba (rhymes with "ha!")	—	בָּ
va	—	בָ
va	—	בָ
ba	—	בָּ
va	—	בָ
ba	—	בָּ

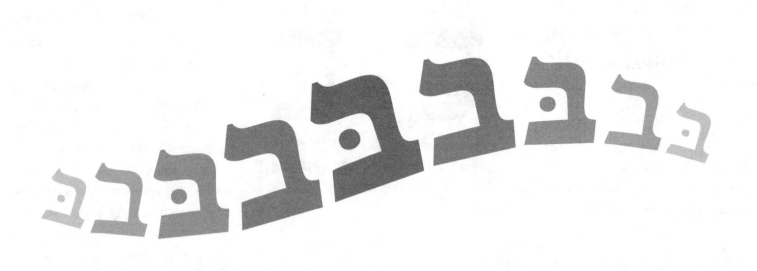

Commentators' Corner

The ת is the first letter of the Hebrew word *Torah*. The Torah is the title for the first five books of the Hebrew Bible, which are often called in English "the Five Books of Moses," since tradition ascribes authorship of the Torah to Moses. The word *Torah*, though often translated as "Law," actually comes from the same Hebrew root found in the word for "teacher." A better translation of the word *Torah* is "teaching" or "instruction." The Torah is the first of the three sections of the Hebrew Bible: *Torah*, *N'vi-im* (Prophets), and *K'tuvim* (Writings). In Hebrew, the first letters of each of these words produce an acronym (*TNK*), pronounced *Tanach*, which is the Hebrew name for the Bible. In what ways can Torah act as our teacher?

Exercises

Remember Hebrew is read from right to left.

תָ תַ תָ

בַּת תָב בַּת

(See back for answers.)

The letter *tav*

sounds like

T

Vital Vowels

Note: Hebrew vowels are usually placed beneath the consonant.

Patach:

The *patach* makes an "ah" sound, like in the English words "FAther" or "BOther." It looks like a tongue depressor, when the doctor makes you say, "AHHHHHHHHH!" In transliteration, it is denoted by the letter *a*. It has the same sound as the *kamatz* vowel:

T'filah Tidbits

The Hebrew word *t'filah* means "prayer" and begins with the letter ת. Interestingly, *t'filah* comes from the Hebrew word *l'hitpaleil*, "to place one's self in judgment." The central set of prayers of the prayer service, the *Amidah* (the prayer we say while "standing"), is referred to as *HaT'filah*, or "The Prayer." In what way does the action of prayer help one to place one's self in judgment?

Transliteration and Answer Key	תַּרְגוּם Translation	תַּרְגִּילִים בְּעִבְרִית Hebrew Exercises
ta	—	תָ
ta	—	תַ
ta	—	תָ
bat	daughter [of]	בַּת
tav	—	תָב
vat (rhymes with "hot")	—	בַת

Commentators' Corner

The שׂ is often inscribed on mezuzot and tefillin (phylacteries) so as to allude to one of the names ascribed to God: *El Shaddai*; *Shaddai* begins with the letter שׁ. Though generally translated as "Almighty," no one knows for certain what this title, *El Shaddai*, means. Some speculate that it means "Mountain God," since Moses first encountered God on Mount Horeb/Sinai. Others even claim that *Shaddai* is an allusion to an ancient notion of God as goddess. The Hebrew word *shadayim* means "breasts," and thus *El Shaddai* (they suggest) means "God of the breasts." Do you ascribe (even without meaning to) a gender to God? Why or why not?

Exercises

Remember Hebrew is read from right to left.

תָ שֶׁ שׁוֹ

בַּת שַׁבָּת

(See back for answers and for more exercises.)

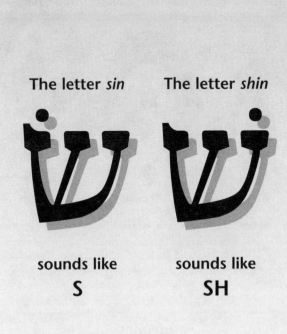

The letter *sin*

The letter *shin*

sounds like
S

sounds like
SH

Vital Vowels

Note: Though Hebrew vowels are usually placed beneath the consonant, this vowel is an exception.

Cholam malei: וֹ

The *cholam* makes a long "o" sound, such as in the words "toad," "code," or "road." It is denoted in transliteration as the letter *o*.

Cholam chaseir: ⬛

Sometimes, the whole *cholam* is not written. Instead a *dageish* (dot) appears between letters to signify the *cholam*. When this *dageish* appears, it also makes the long "o" sound.

T'filah Tidbits

The שׁ is the first letter of the Hebrew word *Shabbat*, שַׁבָּת, which comes from the verb *lishbot*, "to rest." On the seventh day of Creation God rested, and in commemoration of both Creation and the Exodus from Egypt, we rest as well. Based on passages in the Torah, the Sages deduced thirty-nine categories of work that may not be done on שַׁבָּת, so that we may truly rest. (Take note that cooking and cleaning are definitely on that list of prohibitions!) In what ways do you make שַׁבָּת a day of rest for yourself and your family?

Transliteration and Answer Key*	תַּרְגּוּם Translation	תַּרְגִּילִים בְּעִבְרִית Hebrew Exercises
sho	—	שׁוֹ
sa	—	שַׂ
ta	—	תָ
bat (rhymes with "not")	daughter [of]	בַּת
Sha**bbat**	Sabbath	שַׁבָּת
tav	—	תָב
tabas	—	תַבָּשׁ

*For words with more than one syllable, the **accented** syllable is denoted in the transliteration by **bold type**.

Commentators' Corner

The name Moses, or מֹשֶׁה (Mosheh), begins with the letter מ. It appears for the first time in Exodus 2:10. Moses is given the name by Pharaoh's daughter, who explains the name to mean, "I drew him out of the water." Some scholars agree with the Egyptian etymology of this name but are puzzled by its selection. These scholars claim that the verbal root of the name Mosheh means "born" and is generally linked with the name of a god (thus, Rameses means "the god Ra is born"). Perhaps Moses's name was linked originally with a divine name that was later removed. (For further discussion on this, see Carol A. Redmount, "Bitter Lives," *The Oxford History of the Biblical World* [New York: Oxford University Press, 1998], 88–89.)

Exercises

Remember Hebrew is read from right to left.

מֶ מָ מַ

בַּת שַׁבָּת

מֵת תֶם בֶּם

(See back for answers.)

The letter *mem*

sounds like
M

When the letter מ is the last letter of a word, it is called a final *mem* or, in Hebrew, *mem sofit*.

The letter *mem sofit*

also sounds like
M

Vital Vowels

Note: Hebrew vowels are usually placed beneath the consonant.

Segol: ◻

The *segol* makes a short "e" sound, such as in the words "bed," "head," or "elephant." In transliteration, it is denoted by the letter *e*.

T'filah Tidbits

The first prayers of the main body of the service are the *Bar'chu* and the blessing for Creation, both prayers that start with the letter ב. The next segment of the prayer service deals with revelation, which focuses on the mutual love between God and the people Israel. The Hebrew word for "love," *ahavah*, begins with the letter *aleph*, א. The third segment of the service deals with redemption. This concept is epitomized by the quotation from the Israelites' "Song of the Sea" in the Book of Exodus. Having just crossed the parted sea onto dry land, our ancestors sang, *Mi chamochah ba-eilim Adonai?*... "Who is like You, O God, among the gods that are worshipped? Who is like You, gloried in holiness, extolled in praises, working wonders?" The first word of this song is *mi*, which means "who?" It begins with the letter מ. When you imagine the concept of redemption, what do you picture?

Transliteration and Answer Key*	תַּרְגּוּם Translation	תַּרְגִּילִים בְּעִבְרִית Hebrew Exercises
me (the "e" sounds like "men")	—	מֶ
ma	—	מָ
ma	—	מַ
bat	daughter	בַּת
Sha**bbat**	Sabbath	שַׁבָּת
met	—	מֶת
tam (rhymes with "mom")	a simpleton	תָּם
bam (rhymes with "mom")	—	בַּם

*For words with more than one syllable, the **accented** syllable is denoted in the transliteration by **bold type**.

Commentators' Corner

The ל is the second letter of the Hebrew word shalom, שָׁלוֹם. The root of shalom is שׁ־ל־מ, shaleim, meaning "wholeness." In Modern Hebrew, שָׁלוֹם has developed several meanings. It is a greeting of welcome and a salutation of departure, as well as the Hebrew word for "peace." On Shabbat, שַׁבָּת, we wish each other a Shabbat Shalom, שָׁלוֹם שַׁבָּת, "Sabbath of peace, a Sabbath of spiritual wholeness." How does שַׁבָּת lead to a sense of wholeness?

Exercises

Remember Hebrew is read from right to left.

לֶ שֶׁ לְ

לֵב בָּל שָׁלֵם

שַׁבָּת שָׁלוֹם

(See back for answers and for more exercises.)

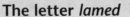

The letter *lamed*

sounds like

L

Vital Vowels

Note: Hebrew vowels are usually placed beneath the consonant.

Tzeirei: ⬜

The *tzeirei* makes a long "a" sound, such as in the words "hay," "day," or "weigh." In transliteration, it is usually denoted by the letters *ei*.

T'filah Tidbits

The ל is the first letter of the Hebrew prayer *L'chah Dodi*. This is sung in the middle of the *Kabbalat Shabbat* (קַבָּלַת שַׁבָּת) service in order to usher in the metaphorical "Sabbath bride." *L'chah Dodi* was written in the sixteenth century by Rabbi Shlomo Alkabetz, one of the kabbalists (Jewish mystics) in the Israeli city of Safed. If you put together the first letter of each stanza of *L'chah Dodi*, not counting the chorus, it is an acrostic in which the author spells out his own name.

Transliteration and Answer Key*	תַּרְגּוּם Translation	תַּרְגִּילִים בְּעִבְרִית Hebrew Exercises
lei (rhymes with "hey")	—	לֵ
shei	—	שֵׁ
le	—	לְ
leiv	heart	לֵב
bal	—	בָּל
sha**leim**	complete	שָׁלֵם
Sha**bbat** sha**lom**	*Shabbat shalom!* Have a peaceful Sabbath!	שַׁבָּת שָׁלוֹם
sheim	name	שֵׁם
bat	daughter	בַּת

*For words with more than one syllable, the **accented** syllable is denoted in the transliteration by **bold type**.

Commentators' Corner

The ר is the first letter of the word for "healer," *rofei*. The notion of God as a healer is very ancient. One of the first prayers actually mentioned in the Bible is Moses's request for Miriam to be cured of leprosy. The prophet says simply, "Please, God, heal her." Today we continue this notion of God as a healer, both in the *Mi Shebeirach* prayer and during the weekday *Amidah*. How do you understand the idea of God as healer?

Exercises

Remember Hebrew is read from right to left.

לְ שֶׁ רְ

רֹשׁ שָׁמוֹר

שׁוֹמֵר שָׁלוֹם

(See back for answers and for more exercises.)

The letter *reish*

sounds like

R

Vital Vowels

Note: Hebrew vowels are usually placed beneath the consonant.

Sh'va: ▪

The *sh'va* is a vowel that functions in two ways. When the *sh'va* appears beneath the first letter of a word (as well as at some other times not covered here), it makes the sound of "i," as in "sit" or "hit." Otherwise, the *sh'va* is a silent vowel. In transliteration, the pronounced *sh'va* is often denoted by an apostrophe.

T'filah Tidbits

One of the concluding blessings of the *Amidah* is the "Worship" prayer, in which the first word is *r'tzei*, "receive." In this prayer we ask God to favorably receive our prayers, and the traditional prayer calls for a return to Zion and restoration of the Holy Temple of Jerusalem as well. The Reform Movement removes references to restoration of the sacrificial cult, because it believes that this practice had a place in our historical past but not our future. However, Reform liturgy maintains the commitment to Zion and our praise of God for accepting our worship. How do you relate to the ancient Jewish connection with the land of Zion and Jerusalem? Why do you think it was important for the early liturgists to include these references in our prayers?

Transliteration and Answer Key*	תַּרְגּוּם Translation	תַּרְגִּילִים בְּעִבְרִית Hebrew Exercises
r'	—	רְ
sh'	—	שְׁ
lei	—	לֵ
rosh	—	רֹשׁ
sha**mor**	keep	שָׁמוֹר
shomeir	keeper	שׁוֹמֵר
sha**lom**	hello, good-bye, peace	שָׁלוֹם
sim sha**lom**	Grant peace!	שִׂים שָׁלוֹם
Sha**bbat** sha**lom**	*Shabbat shalom!* Have a peaceful Sabbath!	שַׁבָּת שָׁלוֹם

*For words with more than one syllable, the **accented** syllable is denoted in the transliteration by **bold type**.

Commentators' Corner

On Saturday night, when שַׁבָּת has come to an end, it's time for *Havdalah* (הַבְדָּלָה). The word הַבְדָּלָה means "separation" and refers to the symbolic separation of the holiness of שַׁבָּת from the rest of the week. Traditionally, blessings are made over wine, spices, and the fire of a candle, and the ceremony then concludes with the specific הַבְדָּלָה blessing. The wine symbolizes the joy of שַׁבָּת; the spices provide comfort over the passing of שַׁבָּת; the illumination from the candle both comforts us in the darkness of the evening and reminds us that Adam was first given fire on שַׁבָּת (*B'reishit Rabbah* 11:2). Have you ever performed a הַבְדָּלָה ceremony at home? Have you ever seen *Havdalah* done at the synagogue?

Exercises

Remember Hebrew is read from right to left.

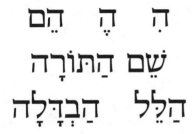

(See back for answers and for more exercises.)

The letter *hei*

ה

sounds like

H

when accompanied by a vowel or beginning a syllable. Otherwise, it's silent!

Vital Vowels

Note: Hebrew vowels are usually placed beneath the consonant.

Chirik: ִ

The *chirik* makes a long "e" sound, like in the English words "tree" or "bee." In transliteration, it is usually denoted by the letter *i*.

Note: In Hebrew, there is no letter or pair of letters that are the equivalent of the English combination "ch" (as in chip). Though in transliteration you may see the letters *ch*, they represent a deep guttural sound akin to clearing your throat, as in *challah*, the bread we eat on שַׁבָּת, or as in "Bach."

T'filah Tidbits

Immediately following the morning *Amidah* on Passover, Shavuot, and Sukkot, as well as on Chanukah and Rosh Chodesh, six specific psalms are recited. The Talmud relates that the prophets declared that hymns of praise should be offered whenever we commemorate our deliverance from peril. The Sages thus ordained six psalms (attributed to King David) that fulfill this obligation. Psalms 113–118 are therefore known collectively as *Hallel*, הַלֵּל, "Hymns of Praise."

The letter ה is also found throughout the prayer book and Bible as a prefix. Used this way, ה means "the."

Transliteration and Answer Key*	תַּרְגוּם Translation	תַּרְגִּילִים בְּעִבְרִית Hebrew Exercises
hi (sounds like "hee")	—	הִ
he (as in "head")	—	הֶ
heim	they (masculine or mixed gender)	הֵם
sheim	name	שֵׁם
haTo**rah**	the Torah	הַתּוֹרָה
Ha**lleil**	Psalms of Praise	הַלֵּל
Havda**lah**	separation	הַבְדָּלָה
shomeir	keeper	שׁוֹמֵר
shomeir Sha**bbat**	keeper of the Sabbath	שׁוֹמֵר שַׁבָּת
To**rah**	Torah, instruction	תּוֹרָה
leiv	heart	לֵב

*For words with more than one syllable, the **accented** syllable is denoted in the transliteration by **bold type**.

Commentators' Corner

According to a midrash (Jewish legend), the א complained before God for twenty-six generations: "Sovereign of the universe! I am the first of the letters, yet You did not create the world with me!" (see Commentators' Corner for the letter ב). God finally answered the א while the Hebrews were wandering in the desert: "The world and everything in it were created for the sake of the Torah alone. Tomorrow, when I come to reveal My Torah and Ten Commandments at Sinai, I will start with none but you: I, the Eternal, am your God, [Exodus 20:2]." The Hebrew word *anochi*, which means "I," is the first word of the Ten Commandments and begins with the letter א. Why do you think this is the first statement?

Exercises

Remember Hebrew is read from right to left.

אוּ   אֶ   אַ

בָּא   אַבָּא   אָב

אִמָּא   הוּא

(See back for answers and for more exercises.)

The letter *aleph*

sounds like...

(nothing! It's a silent letter!)

Vital Vowels

Note: Though Hebrew vowels are usually placed beneath the consonant, this vowel is an exception.

Shuruk: וּ

The *shuruk* makes an "oo" sound, such as in the words "moo," "tuna," or "rooster." In transliteration, it is denoted by the letter *u*.

T'filah Tidbits

The letter א is the first letter of the Hebrew word *ahavah*, which means "love." *Ahavah* is used in two key places in the prayer service. The first part of the main prayer service begins with a call to worship, and a prayer about Creation. Both of these prayers begin with the letter ב. Immediately following the prayer about Creation is a reading on revelation. Revelation is understood traditionally as the process through which God, as an act of love (*ahavah*), revealed Torah to the people Israel. This prayer, *Ahavat Olam* for evenings and *Ahavah Rabbah* for mornings, begins with the letter א and the Hebrew word *ahavah*. After this prayer, we recite the *Shema* and the *V'ahavta*. The *V'ahavta* ("and you shall love") prayer teaches how the people Israel can love God in return. How can we show our love for God?

Transliteration and Answer Key*	תַּרְגוּם Translation	תַּרְגִילִים בְּעִבְרִית Hebrew Exercises
a	—	אַ
e	—	אֶ
u	—	אוּ
av	father (in old Hebrew)	אָב
aba	father (in Aramaic and Modern Hebrew)	אַבָּא
ba	is coming (masculine conjugation)	בָּא
ima	mother (in Aramaic and Modern Hebrew)	אִמָּא
hu	him	הוּא
ba	—	בְּ
at (rhymes with "hot")	you (feminine singular)	אַת
at **i**ma	You are Mom.	אַת אִמָּא
a**tah**	you (masculine singular)	אַתָּה
aba ba	Dad is coming.	אַבָּא בָּא

*For words with more than one syllable, the **accented** syllable is denoted in the transliteration by **bold type**.

Commentators' Corner

The Hebrew word for "tree" is *eitz* (עֵץ), which begins with the letter עָ. In the prayer service, the Torah is referred to as the "tree of life," the *eitz chayim*, עֵץ חַיִּים. This quotation comes from the Book of Proverbs (3:13–18) where it is used in reference to wisdom: "Happy is the person who find wisdom, the one who attains understanding.... **It is a tree of life for those who hold fast to it, and all its supporters are happy**." How does one attain wisdom? The Sages teach that it is through Torah study, of course! Why do you think wisdom gained through the study of Torah is called a "tree of life"?

Exercises

Remember Hebrew is read from right to left.

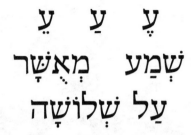

(See back for answers and for more exercises.)

The letter *ayin*
(sounds like "eye" + "in")

sounds like...

(nothing! It's another silent letter!)

Vital Vowels

Note: Hebrew vowels are usually placed beneath the consonant.

Kubutz: ◼

The *kubutz* makes an "oo" sound, such as in the words "moo," "tuna," or "rooster." In transliteration, it is denoted by the letter *u*.

T'filah Tidbits

The word עַל has two meanings. It could mean "on," such as "the book is *on* the table." But it could also mean "is incumbent upon," as in the *Aleinu* prayer, which begins the concluding section of the prayer service. In the *Aleinu*, we are taught that "it is incumbent upon us to praise the God of all things." Ascribed to the Babylonian author Rav in the third century C.E., the *Aleinu* traditionally has two paragraphs. The first paragraph recognizes the chosenness of the Jewish people and the unity of God. The second paragraph looks forward to the day when all the world will uphold monotheism: *Bayom hahu*, "On that day, the Eternal will be One, and God's Name will be One." Take a look at the English of the *Aleinu* in a prayer book. What does it mean to you?

Transliteration and Answer Key*	תַּרְגּוּם Translation	תַּרְגּילִים בְּעִבְרִית Hebrew Exercises
e	—	עֱ
a	—	עַ
ei	—	עֵ
sh'**ma**	Listen!	שְׁמַע
m'u**shar**	happy	מְאֻשָּׁר
al	on, upon, incumbent upon	עַל
sh'lo**shah**	three	שְׁלוֹשָׁה
hu	him	הוּא
heim	them	הֵם
o**lam**	world, universe	עוֹלָם

*For words with more than one syllable, the **accented** syllable is denoted in the transliteration by **bold type**.

Commentators' Corner

The שַׁבָּת candles (singular: נֵר; plural: נֵרוֹת) are lit prior to the start of שַׁבָּת. The prophet Isaiah (58:13–14) declared, "If you proclaim the Sabbath a delight...then you can seek the favor of *Adonai*." Rashi explains that lighting candles on שַׁבָּת brightens the festive meal, thereby making it a delight, and fulfilling the words of Isaiah. Why is the act of lighting the שַׁבָּת candles such a powerful ritual?

Exercises

Remember Hebrew is read from right to left.

נְ　נוּן　נָ

נֵר　נֵרוֹת

נֵר שֶׁל שַׁבָּת

(See back for answers and for more exercises.)

The letter *nun*

sounds like

N

When the letter נ is the last letter of a word, it is called a final *nun* or, in Hebrew, *nun sofit*.

The letter *nun sofit*

also sounds like

N

Vital Vowels

Note: Hebrew vowels are usually placed beneath the consonant.

Chataf patach: ▩

The *chataf patach* makes the same sound as the *patach*: ▩, an "ah" sound, like in the English words "FAther" or "BOther."

T'filah Tidbits

The *Ashrei* is a prayer traditionally said three times a day. Composed of excerpts from Psalms 84:5, 144:15, and 145, it is written as an acrostic poem praising God and all of God's deeds. However, the letter נ is missing from the acrostic! The Talmud claims that the נ may suggest the Hebrew word *naflah*, which means "fallen," as an allusion to the fall of Israel. The Psalmist may have wished to avoid such a reference. Our Rabbis also tell us that one who says the *Ashrei* three times a day has a place in the world-to-come. Why do you think they would have said this?

Transliteration and Answer Key*	תַּרְגּוּם Translation	תַּרְגִּילִים בְּעִבְרִית Hebrew Exercises
n'	—	נְ
nun	—	נוּן
ne	—	נֶ
neir	candle	נֵר
nei**rot**	candles	נֵרוֹת
neir shel Sha**bbat**	candle of the Sabbath (Sabbath candle)	נֵר שֶׁל שַׁבָּת
mata**nah**	gift	מַתָּנָה
Iv**rit**	Hebrew	עִבְרִית
bat (rhymes with "not")	daughter	בַּת
ben	son	בֵּן
a**tem**	you (masculine plural)	אַתֶּם
a**ten**	you (feminine plural)	אַתֶּן
a**mein**	Amen! (I agree!)	אָמֵן

*For words with more than one syllable, the **accented** syllable is denoted in the transliteration by **bold type**.

Commentators' Corner

The Hebrew word for "conquer" is *kovesh*, which begins with a כ. In *Pirkei Avot*, our Sages ask, "Who is a hero?" The answer is, "One who *conquers* his or her own inner impulses to do evil or selfish acts." They also ask, "And who is rich? One who is content with his lot." How do these statements apply to you? Are you a hero? Are you rich?

Exercises

Remember Hebrew is read from right to left.

כֶּ   כָּ   כְּ

בְּרָכָה   כֹּל

נָכוֹן   אָרוֹן

(See back for answers and for more exercises.)

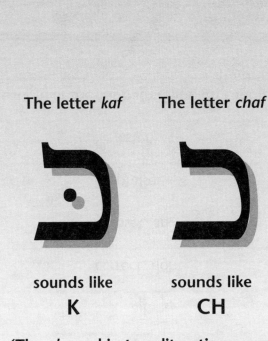

The letter *kaf*   **The letter *chaf***

sounds like   **sounds like**

K   **CH**

(The *ch* used in transliteration represents a deep guttural sound akin to clearing your throat, as in the bread we eat on שַׁבָּת, "challah," or in the name "Bach.")

Vital Vowels

Note: Hebrew vowels are usually placed beneath the consonant.

Chataf kamatz: ◌ֳ

The *chataf kamatz* makes a long "o" sound, such as in the words "toad," "code," or "road."

T'filah Tidbits

When we remove the Torah from the ark during the Torah service, we chant, *Ki miTziyon teitzei Torah, ud'var Adonai mirushalayim,* "For from out of Zion will come the Torah, and the word of the Eternal from Jerusalem." This quotation, from Isaiah 2:3, begins with the letter כ. Why is Israel thought to be the place from which Torah and the word of God will come forth?

Transliteration and Answer Key*	תַּרְגּוּם Translation	תַּרְגִּילִים בְּעִבְרִית Hebrew Exercises
ki	—	כְּ
chi	—	כְ
kei	—	כֵּ
ki	because, for	כִּי
b'ra**chah**	blessing	בְּרָכָה
kol	all	כֹּל
na**chon**	correct, right	נָכוֹן
a**ron**	closet, ark	אָרוֹן
bar'**chu**	praise!	בָּרְכוּ
sh'**ma**	listen!	שְׁמַע
neir shel sha**bbat**	candle of the Sabbath (Sabbath candle)	נֵר שֶׁל שַׁבָּת
nesher	eagle	נֶשֶׁר

*For words with more than one syllable, the **accented** syllable is denoted in the transliteration by **bold type**.

Commentators' Corner

The Hebrew word *chai*, חַי, means "lives," as in *David melech Yisrael, chai, chai, v'kayam*, "David, king of Israel, lives, lives, and endures." The two Hebrew letters that spell the word *chai* are ח and י. Each Hebrew letter has a numerical equivalent, and the sum of the ח (the 8th letter) and י (the 10th letter) is 18 (ח = 8, י = 10). As a result of this association between 18 and the word *chai*, "life," the number 18 has become a symbol of luck and even protection within Jewish communities around the world. It is common to see people wearing necklaces or other jewelry with the word חַי, and often monetary donations or gifts are offered in increments of 18.

Exercises

Remember Hebrew is read from right to left.

(See back for answers and for more exercises.)

The letter *chet*

sounds like

CH

(The *ch* used in transliteration represents a deep guttural sound akin to clearing your throat, as in the bread we eat on שַׁבָּת, "challah," or in the name "Bach.")

Vital Vowels

Note: Hebrew vowels are usually placed beneath the consonant.

When a Hebrew letter has the vowel *patach* underneath it and that letter is followed by a י, the combination of vowels makes the sound of a long "i," like in the words "fly," "kite," "bike," or *chai*, חַי. In transliteration, it is denoted by the letters *ai*.

T'filah Tidbits

When moving into a new house or apartment, we can perform an act called *chanukat habayit*, "dedication of a home." This is like a Jewish housewarming. The word חֲנֻכָּה, *chanukah*, meaning "dedication," begins with the letter ח. As part of this act of dedicating a home, we hang a mezuzah and say the blessing, "Blessed are You, *Adonai* our God, Sovereign of the Universe, who commands us to affix the mezuzah." Thus the house or apartment becomes a Jewish home! Why do you think the holiday that begins on the 25th day of (the Hebrew month of) Kislev is called "Chanukah"?

Transliteration and Answer Key*	תַּרְגוּם Translation	תַּרְגִּילִים בְּעִבְרִית Hebrew Exercises
cha	—	חַ
cha	—	חָ
chai (rhymes with "buy")	life, lives	חַי
ach	brother	אָח
chag	festival, holiday	חַג
lechem	bread	לֶחֶם
a**chot**	sister	אָחוֹת
Chanu**kah**	Chanukah (dedication)	חֲנֻכָּה
b'ra**chah**	blessing	בְּרָכָה
To**rah**	Torah (instruction)	תּוֹרָה
aha**vah**	love	אַהֲבָה
aha**vat** o**lam**	love of the world (name of the prayer that precedes the *Shema* in the evening service)	אַהֲבַת עוֹלָם
aha**vah** ra**bbah**	abounding love (name of the prayer that precedes the *Shema* in the morning service)	אַהֲבָה רַבָּה

*For words with more than one syllable, the **accented** syllable is denoted in the transliteration by **bold type**.

Commentators' Corner

When used as a prefix with a noun, the וֹ indicates either the conjunction "and" or the disjunction "but"; attached to a verb, the וֹ can indicate the imperfect tense. For example, the expression אַבָּא וְאִמָּא means "father *and* mother."

The letter *vav*

sounds like

V

Exercises

Remember Hebrew is read from right to left.

וֹ וִ וַ

וְאָהַבְתָּ וְשָׁמְרוּ

וְנֶאֱמַר עוֹלָם

(See back for answers and for more exercises.)

Vital Vowels

Note: Hebrew vowels are usually placed beneath the consonant.

Chataf segol:

The *chataf segol* makes the same sound as the *segol*: a short "e" sound, such as in the words "bed," "head," or "elephant."

T'filah Tidbits

The וֹ is familiar as the first letter of the *V'shamru*, וְשָׁמְרוּ. וְשָׁמְרוּ is a quotation from Exodus 31:16–17 that is read or sung on both Friday nights and Saturday mornings. It teaches us that the שַׁבָּת is a reminder that God created the world in six days and rested on the seventh, thus we are to *keep* or *guard* שַׁבָּת. In other words, if even God needed a day off once a week, so do we! Those who observe שַׁבָּת according to the strictest interpretation of the traditional laws are called שׁוֹמֵר שַׁבָּת. However, there are many ways to remember the specialness of שַׁבָּת. In what ways do you personally observe שַׁבָּת as a sign from God? What do you do to make שַׁבָּת special and set apart from the rest of the week?

Transliteration and Answer Key*	תַּרְגּוּם Translation	תַּרְגִּילִים בְּעִבְרִית Hebrew Exercises
vi	—	וִ
v'	and	וְ
va	—	וַ
v'ahav**ta**	and you shall love	וְאָהַבְתָּ
v'sham**ru**	And they [the children of Israel] shall keep	וְשָׁמְרוּ
v'ne-e**mar**	and it is said	וְנֶאֱמַר
o**lam**	world, universe	עוֹלָם
neir shel Sha**bbat**	Sabbath candle	נֵר שֶׁל שַׁבָּת
v'**hu**	and he	וְהוּא
l'o**lam** va-**ed**	forever	לְעוֹלָם וָעֶד
ba**yom** ha**hu**	on that day	בַּיּוֹם הַהוּא
To**rah**	Torah	תּוֹרָה

*For words with more than one syllable, the **accented** syllable is denoted in the transliteration by **bold type**.

Commentators' Corner

In Exodus, God reveals the Divine Name to Moses, characterized by a four-letter word whose root reflects the verb "to be" (Exodus 3:14). According to tradition, only the High Priest of Israel knew how to pronounce God's name. When the Holy Temple of Jerusalem was destroyed (the First Temple in 586 B.C.E. by the Babylonians, and the Second Temple in 70 C.E. by the Romans) and the priesthood came to an end, knowledge of the proper pronunciation of God's name was lost. Today, the name of God is abbreviated in our prayer books as יי, which is read as *Adonai* and may be translated as "my Master."

Exercises

Remember Hebrew is read from right to left.

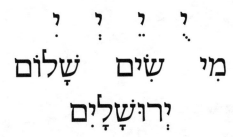

(See back for answers and for more exercises.)

Vital Vowels

CONGRATULATIONS! YOU'VE LEARNED ALL OF THE VOWELS!

The letter *yod*

sounds like

Y

when accompanied by a vowel or beginning a syllable.

Otherwise, it's silent!

T'filah Tidbits

The central set of prayers in the prayer service, called the *Amidah* or *HaT'filah*, is often concluded by the reciting of *Yihyu L'ratzon*. This prayer, which begins with the Hebrew letter י, asks that the words of our mouth and the meditations of our hearts be acceptable to God. It is attributed in the Talmud to Mar son of Rabina. When you address God directly, for what do you pray?

Transliteration and Answer Key*	תַּרְגּוּם Translation	תַּרְגִּילִים בְּעִבְרִית Hebrew Exercises
yu	—	יֻ
yei	—	יֵ
y'	—	יְ
yi	—	יִ
mi	who	מִי
sim sha**lom**	Grant peace!	שִׂים שָׁלוֹם
Y'rusha**la**yim	Jerusalem	יְרוּשָׁלַיִם
Yisra-**eil**	Israel	יִשְׂרָאֵל
hala**chah**	Jewish law	הֲלָכָה
Elo**hei**nu	our God	אֱלֹהֵינוּ
hal'lu**yah**	Praise God! Hallelujah!	הַלְלוּיָהּ
ish	man	אִישׁ
i**shah**	woman	אִשָּׁה

*For words with more than one syllable, the **accented** syllable is denoted in the transliteration by **bold type**.

Commentators' Corner

Scholars believe that the earliest written alphabet comes from the Middle East. In this ancient alphabet, which lasted for many generations, the ד is represented as a fish, because the Hebrew word for fish is *dag*, דָּג. However, the letter ד later became associated with *delet*, דֶּלֶת, "door," and thus we have our Hebrew letter for the "D" sound. Can you see the "door" in the ד? The English letter "D" actually comes from the original picture of the fish. Can you see a fish in the "D"?

The letter *dalet*

sounds like

D

Vital Vowels—Review

Note: Though Hebrew vowels are usually placed beneath the consonant, this vowel is an exception.

Shuruk: וּ

The *shuruk* makes an "oo" sound, such as in the words "moo," "tuna," or "rooster." In transliteration, it is usually denoted by the letter *u*.

Exercises

Remember Hebrew is read from right to left.

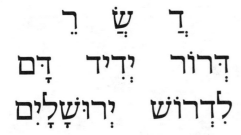

(See back for answers and for more exercises.)

T'filah Tidbits

The word "sermon" may be rendered in Hebrew as either דְּבַר תּוֹרָה *d'var Torah* —literally, "a word of Torah"—or דְּרָשָׁה, *d'rashah*, both beginning with the letter ד. The expression *d'rashah* comes from the biblical verb *lidrosh*, used in relation to Ezra the scribe *explaining* the Torah to the people (Ezra 7:10).

Transliteration and Answer Key*	תַּרְגּוּם Translation	תַּרְגִּילִים בְּעִבְרִית Hebrew Exercises
da	—	דַּ
sa	—	שֶׂ
rei	—	רֵ
d'**ror**	liberty, freedom; sparrow	דְּרוֹר
y'**did**	friend	יְדִיד
dam	blood	דָּם
lid**rosh**	to search out	לִדְרוֹשׁ
Y'rusha**la**yim	Jerusalem	יְרוּשָׁלַיִם
chag	festival, holiday	חַג
lechem	bread	לֶחֶם
yal**dah**	girl	יַלְדָּה
yeled	boy	יֶלֶד
sim sha**lom**	Grant peace!	שִׂים שָׁלוֹם

*For words with more than one syllable, the **accented** syllable is denoted in the transliteration by **bold type**.

Commentators' Corner

The fringes on the four corners of a tallit are called tzitzit, צִיצִית. In the Book of Numbers, we are commanded to wear צִיצִית, fringes, in order to remember God's commandments. Furthermore, according to the medieval rabbi Rashi, the eight strands of the צִיצִית represent the eight days between the Israelites beginning the Exodus and the Song of the Sea. The five knots symbolize the Pentateuch, or Five Books of Moses. Thirty-nine rings are wrapped around the צִיצִית, which correspond to the numerical value of the Hebrew יי אֶחָד, "Adonai is One."

Exercises

Remember Hebrew is read from right to left.

צֶ יוֹ צִ

צוֹם צִיצִית

יְצִיאַת מִצְרַיִם

(See back for answers and for more exercises.)

The letter *tzadi*

sounds like
TZ
(as in leT'S)

When the letter צ is the last letter of a word, it is called a final *tzadi* or, in Hebrew, *tzadi sofit*.

The letter *tzadi sofit*

also sounds like
TZ

Vital Vowels—Review

Note: Hebrew vowels are usually placed beneath the consonant.

Chirik: ▪

The *chirik* makes a long "e" sound, like in the English words "tree" or "bee" and in the Hebrew word מִי.

T'filah Tidbits

Psalm 92, found in the traditional *Kabbalat Shabbat* (קַבָּלַת שַׁבָּת) liturgy, relates, *Tzaddik katamar yifrach, k'erez balvanon yisgeh,* "A righteous person will flourish like a date palm [*tamar*], like a cedar [*erez*] in Lebanon s/he will grow tall." In Hebrew, a righteous person is called a *tzaddik*, which begins with the letter צ. Likewise, an act of righteousness is called *tzedakah*, which also begins with a צ. People often translate *tzedakah* as "charity." What is the difference between the two translations, "charity" and "righteousness"? What, if anything, is the significance of the difference?

Transliteration and Answer Key*	תַּרְגּוּם Translation	תַּרְגִּילִים בְּעִבְרִית Hebrew Exercises
tzei	—	צֵ
yo	—	יוֹ
tzi	—	צִ
tzom	fast (as in "not eating")	צוֹם
tzi**tzit**	fringes (especially with regard to fringes of a tallit, prayer shawl)	צִיצִית
Mitz**ra**yim	Egypt	מִצְרַיִם
y'tzi**at** Mitz**ra**yim	the Exodus from Egypt	יְצִיאַת מִצְרַיִם
za**chor**	remember	זְכוֹר
mitz**vah**	commandment	מִצְוָה
Bir**kat** Ha**Ch**odesh	Blessing of the [New] Month	בִּרְכַּת הַחוֹדֶשׁ
Sha**bbat** sha**lom**	*Shabbat shalom!* Have a peaceful Sabbath!	שַׁבָּת שָׁלוֹם
lechem	bread	לֶחֶם

*For words with more than one syllable, the **accented** syllable is denoted in the transliteration by **bold type**.

Commentators' Corner

When the Israelites crossed the Reed Sea, they sang a joyous song of celebration called the Song of the Sea. Part of that song became incorporated into our prayer service, known as the *Mi Chamocha* prayer. In it, we praise God, asking who is like God, gloried in holiness, extolled in praises, working wonders. The Hebrew word for wonder is *pele* (פֶּלֶא), or as it is rendered for grammatical reasons in Exodus 15, פֶלֶא. In modern times, the word פֶּלֶא is used for modern-day wonders in addition to those of a more divine nature. For example, a cellular phone in Israel is called a *pela-fon*, "a wonder phone"!

Exercises

Remember Hebrew is read from right to left.

פָ עֶ פֵ

פֶּה רוֹפֵא פִּתְחוּ

שׁוֹמֵר עִבְרִית

(See back for answers and for more exercises.)

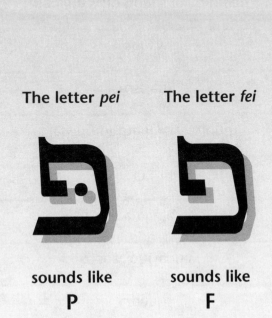

The letter *pei*

פּ

sounds like

P

The letter *fei*

פ

sounds like

F

Vital Vowels

A note about Hebrew grammar

בֶּגֶד כֶּפֶת: The *Beged Kefet* Rule

When one of the six Hebrew letters above begins a word or follows a closed syllable, it receives a *dageish* (dot on the inside). Thus the word for "house" is not *vayit* (בַיִת), but rather *bayit* (בַּיִת), because the בּ comes at the beginning of the word. However, this rule is subverted in the Bible or prayer book (but not in Modern Hebrew) if any of these בֶּגֶד כֶּפֶת letters are preceded by any of the following letters: י, ו, ה, א. When a word ends with א, ה, ו, י, they act to open the syllable, turning off the בֶּגֶד כֶּפֶת rule. Thus, we read עוֹשֵׂה פֶלֶא instead of עוֹשֵׂה פֶּלֶא.

T'filah Tidbits

Especially during the *N'ilah* (concluding) services on Yom Kippur, and sometimes at other points in the service as well, we ask God to open the gates of righteousness for us. This request "to open" is written פִּתְחוּ. It is a quotation from Psalm 118:19: *Pitchu li shaarei tzedek; avo vam odeh Yah,* "Open for me the gates of righteousness; I will enter them and praise the Eternal One."

Transliteration and Answer Key*	תַּרְגּוּם Translation	תַּרְגִּילִים בְּעִבְרִית Hebrew Exercises
pa	—	פָּ
i	—	עִ
pei	—	פֵּ
peh	mouth	פֶּה
rofei	healer	רוֹפֵא
pit**chu**	Open!	פִּתְחוּ
sho**meir** Iv**rit**	keeper of Hebrew	שׁוֹמֵר עִבְרִית
eitz cha**yim**	tree of life	עֵץ חַיִּים
sh'**ma** Yisra-**eil**	hear, O Israel	שְׁמַע יִשְׂרָאֵל
Bir**kat** Ha**Cho**desh	Blessing of the [New] Month	בִּרְכַּת הַחוֹדֶשׁ
Y'rusha**la**yim	Jerusalem	יְרוּשָׁלַיִם
Iv**rit**	Hebrew	עִבְרִית
ha**mo**tzi **le**chem	the One who brings forth bread	הַמּוֹצִיא לֶחֶם

*For words with more than one syllable, the **accented** syllable is denoted in the transliteration by **bold type**.

Commentators' Corner

On Yom Kippur, we read from Leviticus 19:2 where God tells us, "You shall be holy, for I, *Adonai* your God, am holy." The word for "holy" is *kadosh*, קָדוֹשׁ. The word actually signifies a sense of separation or apartness. Does something have to be separate to be holy? Does something have to be unique to be holy? What does it mean to be holy? This commandment in Leviticus is immediately followed by a list of actions that, if followed properly, could make us holy. It includes, but is not limited to, honoring one's parents, observing Shabbat, providing for the poor, stranger, and disabled, and upholding justice.

Exercises

Remember Hebrew is read from right to left.

קֵ   קֵ   קֵ

קְדוּשָׁה   קָדוֹשׁ

כְּבוֹדוֹ   נְקַדֵּשׁ

(See back for answers and for more exercises.)

The letter *kuf*

sounds like

K

Vital Vowels—Review

Note: Hebrew vowels are usually placed beneath the consonant.

Tzeirei: ◌ֵ

The *tzeirei* makes a long "a" sound, such as in the words "hay," "day," or "weigh."

T'filah Tidbits

In the midst of our morning *Amidah*, we find the *K'dushah* (קְדוּשָׁה) (sanctification) prayer. This prayer uses three biblical quotations to proclaim God's holiness. Included is Isaiah's vision of angels who declare, "Holy, Holy, Holy is the Eternal God of Hosts! The earth is full of God's glory" (Isaiah. 6:3). Traditionally, the קְדוּשָׁה is said while standing at attention, feet together. We then rise slightly on our toes at each mention of קָדוֹשׁ, just as Isaiah described the *s'rafim* (angels) who "fluttered about."

Transliteration and Answer Key*	תַּרְגּוּם Translation	תַּרְגִּילִים בְּעִבְרִית Hebrew Exercises
kei	—	קֵ
ka	—	קַ
ku	—	קֻ
ka**dosh**	holy (as an adjective)	קָדוֹשׁ
k'du**shah**	holiness (as a noun)	קְדוּשָׁה
n'ka**deish**	we sanctify	נְקַדֵּשׁ
k'vo**do**	his honor, his glory	כְּבוֹדוֹ
sh'**ma** yisra-**eil**	hear, O Israel	שְׁמַע יִשְׂרָאֵל
neir shel sha**bbat**	Sabbath candle	נֵר שֶׁל שַׁבָּת
eitz cha**yim** hi	it is a tree of life	עֵץ חַיִּים הִיא
hamaa**riv** ara**vim**	the One whose word makes evening fall	הַמַּעֲרִיב עֲרָבִים

*For words with more than one syllable, the **accented** syllable is denoted in the transliteration by **bold type**.

Commentators' Corner

For Ashkenazic Jews (Jews of northeastern and northwestern European descent), a *S'lichot* (סְלִיחוֹת) service is traditionally held on the Saturday night before Rosh HaShanah. This collection of penitential prayers is designed to get us into the appropriate frame of mind for the High Holy Days. The practice of holding this service is over 1,500 years old! Sephardic Jews (Jews of Spanish, Middle Eastern, or North African descent) however, say these prayers every morning at sunrise for the entire month before Rosh HaShanah!

Exercises

Remember Hebrew is read from right to left.

סוּ   סֶ   סְ

סְלִיחוֹת   סְלִיחָה

סְלַח לָנוּ

(See back for answers and for more exercises.)

The letter *samech*

ס

sounds like

S

Vital Vowels—Review

Note: Hebrew vowels are usually placed beneath the consonant.

Segol: ◌ֶ

The *segol* makes a short "e" sound, such as in the words "bed," "head," or "elephant."

T'filah Tidbits

The prayer for forgiveness, סְלִיחָה, is found in the midst of our daily *Amidah*. In it, we recognize our transgressions and ask God for forgiveness. In Modern Hebrew, the word סְלִיחָה has taken on the more everyday connotation of "Excuse me!" It is common in Israel to hear "סְלִיחָה! סְלִיחָה!" as someone elbows his way through a crowd or cuts into a line.

Transliteration and Answer Key*	תַּרְגּוּם Translation	תַּרְגִּילִים בְּעִבְרִית Hebrew Exercises
se	—	סֶ
sei	—	סֵ
su	—	סוּ
s'li**chah**	excuse me!	סְלִיחָה
s'lichot	forgivings	סְלִיחוֹת
s'lach **la**nu	forgive us	סְלַח לָנוּ
v'sham**ru** v'**nei** yisra-**eil**	and the children of Israel shall keep	וְשָׁמְרוּ בְנֵי יִשְׂרָאֵל
hamaa**riv** ara**vim**	the One whose word makes evening fall	הַמַּעֲרִיב עֲרָבִים
a**lei**nu	let us	עָלֵינוּ
laa**sok** b'div**rei** To**rah**	to engage in the words of Torah	לַעֲסוֹק בְּדִבְרֵי תוֹרָה
l'o**lam** va-**ed**	forever	לְעוֹלָם וָעֶד
ba**yom** ha**hu**	on that day	בַּיּוֹם הַהוּא

*For words with more than one syllable, the **accented** syllable is denoted in the transliteration by **bold type**.

Commentators' Corner

The Hebrew word *tallit*, Jewish prayer shawl, begins with the letter ט. In Numbers 15, God commands the Jewish people to attach fringes (*tzitzit*) to any garment with four corners. As the popular custom of wearing four-cornered garments as daily clothing waned, the Sages feared that this commandment would become obsolete. Thus they developed the concept of a four-cornered garment to be worn during morning prayer, and in that way people could still fulfill the commandment.

The letter *tet*

ט

sounds like

T

Exercises

Remember Hebrew is read from right to left.

טֶ טֵ טְ

טַלִּית טוֹב לֶחֶם

אֵל מָלֵא רַחֲמִים

(See back for answers and for more exercises.)

Vital Vowels—Review

Note: Though Hebrew vowels are usually placed beneath the consonant, this vowel is an exception.

Cholam: וֹ

The *cholam* makes a long "o" sound, such as in the words "toad," "code," or "road."

T'filah Tidbits

Psalm 92 tells us that it is good to give thanks to God. The Hebrew word for "good," *tov*, טוֹב, begins with a ט. This psalm is about plucking strings and sounding the lute in praise of the Holy One, and is traditionally read on שַׁבָּת. If this psalm is read on שַׁבָּת, why do Jews traditionally avoid playing instruments on שַׁבָּת? Why do you think the Reform Movement and some Conservative synagogues grant permission to do so?

Transliteration and Answer Key*	תַּרְגּוּם Translation	תַּרְגִּילִים בְּעִבְרִית Hebrew Exercises
to	—	טֶ
ta	—	טֶ
te	—	טְ
ta**llit**	Jewish prayer shawl	טַלִּית
tov	good	טוֹב
lechem	bread	לֶחֶם
Eil ma**lei** racha**mim**	God full of mercy	אֵל מָלֵא רַחֲמִים
Sha**losh** R'ga**lim**	Three Pilgrimage Festivals (Passover, Shavuot, Sukkot)	שָׁלֹשׁ רְגָלִים
dam	blood	דָּם
chag	festival, holiday	חַג
laa**sok** b'div**rei** To**rah**	to engage in the words of Torah	לַעֲסוֹק בְּדִבְרֵי תוֹרָה
sim sha**lom**	Grant peace!	שִׂים שָׁלוֹם

טטטט
טט
ט

*For words with more than one syllable, the **accented** syllable is denoted in the transliteration by **bold type**.

Commentators' Corner

The Hebrew word for "remember" is *zachor*, which begins with a זַ. A list of the Ten Commandments appears three times in the Torah, two of which are nearly identical. The only difference between those two versions, found in Exodus 20 and Deuteronomy 5, is in the commandment to observe שַׁבָּת. In Deuteronomy we are told to keep (שָׁמוֹר) the שַׁבָּת, and in Exodus we are told to remember (זָכוֹר) the שַׁבָּת. The Rabbis reconcile this difference by claiming that God miraculously caused Israel to hear two requirements simultaneously with regard to שַׁבָּת.

Exercises

Remember Hebrew is read from right to left.

זֶ מִי זְ
זְאֵב זוּג זִכָּרוֹן
לְמַעֲשֵׂה בְרֵאשִׁית

(See back for answers and for more exercises.)

The letter *zayin*

sounds like
Z

Vital Vowels—Review

Note: Hebrew vowels are usually placed beneath the consonant.

Kamatz: ⬛

The *kamatz* makes an "ah" sound, like in the English words "FAther" or "BOther," or in the Hebrew word *baruch*.

T'filah Tidbits

On *Erev* שַׁבָּת, we make a special *Kiddush* (sanctification) over wine in order to sanctify שַׁבָּת. Since we are commanded to remember both Creation and the Exodus on שַׁבָּת, we include the expressions *zikaron l'maasei v'reishit*, "as a reminder of the work of Creation," and *zeicher litziat Mitzrayim*, "a remembrance of the Exodus from Egypt." This way we fulfill the double mitzvah of both keeping and remembering שַׁבָּת. What are the different implications of "keeping" and "remembering"?

Transliteration and Answer Key*	תַּרְגוּם Translation	תַּרְגִּילִים בְּעִבְרִית Hebrew Exercises
ze	—	זֶ
mi	who	מִי
zu	—	זֻ
z'eiv	wolf	זְאֵב
zug	couple, partner, pair	זוּג
zar	foreign	זָר
mu**zar**	weird	מוּזָר
sha**lom**	hello, goodbye, peace	שָׁלוֹם
ta**llit**	Jewish prayer shawl	טַלִּית
zikaron l'maasei v'reishit	as a reminder of the work of Creation	זִכָּרוֹן לְמַעֲשֵׂה בְרֵאשִׁית
lechem	bread	לֶחֶם
Eil ma**lei** racha**mim**	God full of mercy	אֵל מָלֵא רַחֲמִים
sim sha**lom**	Grant peace!	שִׂים שָׁלוֹם

*For words with more than one syllable, the **accented** syllable is denoted in the transliteration by **bold type**.

Commentators' Corner

During the Torah service, a quotation from *Pirkei Avot* is often sung: *Al sh'loshah d'varim haolam omeid: al haTorah, v'al haavodah, v'al g'milut chasadim*, "The world is sustained by three things: Torah, worship, and loving deeds." This third foundation by which the world is sustained, "loving deeds," is expressed by the Hebrew words *g'milut* (which begins with a גּ), or "the process of bestowing," and *chasadim*, "righteousness."

Exercises

Remember Hebrew is read from right to left.

גֹּ גֹּו גֹּו

גָּאַל גְּבוֹר

גוֹמֵל גְּמִילוּת

(See back for answers and for more exercises.)

The letter *gimel*

ג

sounds like

G

(as in "go")

Vital Vowels—Review

Note: Hebrew vowels are usually placed beneath the consonant.

Sh'va: ְ

The *sh'va* is a vowel that functions in two ways. When the *sh'va* appears beneath the first letter of a word (as well as at some other times not covered here), it makes the sound of "i," as in "sit" or "hit." Otherwise, the *sh'va* is a silent vowel. In transliteration, the pronounced *sh'va* is often denoted by an apostrophe.

T'filah Tidbits

The *Birkat HaGomeil* (*gomeil* starts with the letter גּ) is a prayer to acknowledge publicly God's saving deed as an act of God's loving-kindness. Traditionally said during the Torah service, the blessing is offered publicly by one who feels a sense of relief from danger and special gratefulness to God. The blessing is most appropriate at the prayer service in the aftermath of an accident, any serious illness, or surgery where one's life may have been in peril. The translation of *Birkat HaGomeil* is: "Blessed are You, Eternal our God, Sovereign of the universe, who has bestowed every goodness upon me." Have you ever felt the need or desire to say such a prayer?

Transliteration and Answer Key*	תַּרְגּוּם Translation	תַּרְגִּילִים בְּעִבְרִית Hebrew Exercises
g'	—	גְּ
gu	—	גּוּ
go	—	גּוֹ
ga**al**	redeemed	גָּאַל
gi**bor**	hero	גִּבּוֹר
go**meil**	benefactor	גוֹמֵל
g'mi**lut**	recompense	גְּמִילוּת
sha**mor**	Keep!	שָׁמוֹר
sim sha**lom**	Grant peace!	שִׂים שָׁלוֹם
g'**ve**ret	Miss, Mrs.	גְּבֶרֶת
mar	Mr.	מַר
bo**rei** p'**ri** ha**ga**fen	Creator of the fruit of the vine	בּוֹרֵא פְּרִי הַגָּפֶן
rom'**mu**	Rejoice!	רוֹמְמוּ

גגגגגג

*For words with more than one syllable, the **accented** syllable is denoted in the transliteration by **bold type**.

Commentators' Corner

Congratulations! You've learned the entire א-ב. Here are some suggestions for further study on Hebrew and Jewish practice:

Klein, Isaac. *A Guide to Jewish Religious Practice.* New York: Jewish Theological Seminary of America, 1979.

Mihaly, Eugene. *A Song to Creation.* Cincinnati: HUC Press, 1975.

Motzkin, Linda. *Aleph Isn't Tough: An Introduction to Hebrew for Adults, Book 1.* New York: UAHC Press, 2000.

— *Aleph Isn't Enough: Hebrew for Adults, Book 2.* New York: UAHC Press, 2001.

— *Bet Is for B'reishit: Hebrew for Adults, Book 3.* New York: UAHC Press, 2004.

— *Tav Is for Torah: Hebrew for Adults, Book 4.* New York: URJ Press, 2005.

Washofsky, Mark. *Jewish Living: A Guide to Reform Jewish Practice.* New York: UAHC Press, 2002.

Exercises

Remember Hebrew is read from right to left.

אַף   אֵיךְ

נוֹף   בָּרוּךְ

הַמְבוֹרָךְ

(See back for answers and for more exercises.)

When the letter כ comes at the end of a word, it is called a *final chaf*, or in Hebrew: *chaf sofit*

It also sounds like
CH

When the letter פ comes at the end of a word, it is called a *final fei*, or in Hebrew: *fei sofit*

It also sounds like
F

Vital Vowels

Note: Hebrew vowels are usually placed beneath the consonant.

Review:

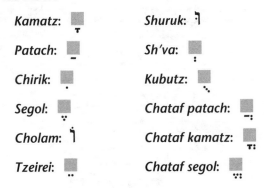

Kamatz: Shuruk:

Patach: Sh'va:

Chirik: Kubutz:

Segol: Chataf patach:

Cholam: Chataf kamatz:

Tzeirei: Chataf segol:

T'filah Tidbits

Congratulations! You've learned the entire א-ב. Here are suggestions for further reading on Jewish prayer:

Donin, Hayim Halevy. *To Pray As a Jew.* New York: Basic Books, 1980.

Fields, Harvey. *B'chol L'vavcha: A Commentary on the Siddur.* New York: UAHC Press, 2001.

Hoffman, Lawrence. *The Way Into Jewish Prayer.* Woodstock, VT: Jewish Lights Publishing, 2000.

Levy, Richard. *A Vision of Holiness: The Future of Reform Judaism.* New York: URJ Press, 2005.

Transliteration and Answer Key*	תַּרְגּוּם Translation	תַּרְגִּילִים בְּעִבְרִית Hebrew Exercises
af	nose	אַף
eich	how?	אֵיךְ
nof	view	נוֹף
ba**ruch**	blessed, praised	בָּרוּךְ
ham'vo**rach**	the blessed One	הַמְבוֹרָךְ
ka**dosh**	holy	קָדוֹשׁ
bo**rei** p'**ri** ha**ga**fen	Creator of the fruit of the vine	בּוֹרֵא פְּרִי הַגָּפֶן
ha**motzi** **le**chem	the One who brings forth bread	הַמּוֹצִיא לֶחֶם
sh'**ma** yisra-**eil**	hear, O Israel	שְׁמַע יִשְׂרָאֵל
neir shel sha**bbat**	Sabbath candle	נֵר שֶׁל שַׁבָּת
eitz cha**yim** hi	it is a tree of life	עֵץ חַיִּים הִיא
mah **to**vu oha**le**cha Yaa**kov**	how lovely are your tents, O Jacob	מַה טֹּבוּ אֹהָלֶיךָ יַעֲקֹב

*For words with more than one syllable, the **accented** syllable is denoted in the transliteration by **bold type**.